Victorian Découpage

FLOWERS

CAXTON EDITIONS

This edition first published in the United Kingdom in 2001 by
Caxton Editions
20 Bloomsbury Street
London WC1B 3JH
a member of the Caxton Publishing Group

© 2000 Caxton Publishing Group

Designed and Produced for Caxton Editions by
Open Door Limited
Rutland, UK

Découpeur and professional advisor: Sue Growcott, Chez Soi Ltd, Stamford
Illustrator: Andrew Shepherd, Art Angle
Photography: Chris Allen, Forum Advertising

Colour separation: GA Graphics Stamford

Title: Victorian Découpage, FLOWERS
ISBN: 1-86019-950-X

Acknowledgments:
With kind thanks to Dover publications for their permission to use images from
some of their copyright free publications:
Full-color Victorian Vignettes and Illustrations, edited by Carol Belanger Grafton
Full-color Floral Vignettes, selected and arranged by Carol Belanger Grafton
Old-Fashioned Vignettes in Full Color, selected by Carol Belanger Grafton
For information on where to purchase these titles and other copyright free publications
from Dover Publications see the Sources and Suppliers section in the back of this book.

Contents

Victorian Flowers

Just now the lilac is in bloom
All before my little room;
And in my flower-beds, I think
Smile the carnation and the pink;
And down the borders, well I know,
The poppy and the pansy blow

Rupert Brooke, 1912

The Victorians were enthusiastic gardeners. They loved the romance of history and were ostentatious when it came to display. As a result they created gardens of true romance, gardens that they were to dream about, write about, sing about and paint about.

New-found botanic knowledge enabled gardeners to work with a much larger palette of plants. As many more varieties became available courtesy of plant hybridization, increased colour and a vast diversity of form came to predominate the borders of Victorian England, especially those of the cottage garden.

A keen observer of domestic garden design was the Victorian garden designer Gertrude Jekyll. 'I have learnt much from the little cottage gardens that help to make our English waysides the prettiest in the temperate world,' Jekyll was to write in one of her numerous journals. 'One can hardly go into the smallest cottage garden without learning or observing something new.'

Jekyll designed some 350 gardens during her long and productive career. She loved colour and would talk of the importance of having a good 'flower-eye'. For her, gardens, and indeed floral displays within the home, would be incomplete without the 'roses, peonies and gladiolus of France, and the tulips and hyacinths of Holland, to say nothing of the hosts of good things raised by our home gardeners.' She was also partial to primroses, lilies, double pink and opium poppies, Lent hellebores and white foxgloves.

But flowers did not stay in the garden. Designers, artists and writers used them liberally too.

The floral wreath perhaps epitomizes early Victorian aesthetic thinking. The Victorians had a passion for embellishment, which often took precedence over form. As a result, anything that could be decorated was decorated – often with a floral motif encircled by a border of flowers and scrolls.

The so-called Aesthetic period of the 1870s and 1880s saw a strong Japanese influence. Here flowers are used, but much more specifically than before. Oscar Wilde was to proclaim the sunflower and the lily as 'the two most perfect models of design, the most naturally adapted for decorative art', his comment reflecting a more precise use of floral form.

The Arts and Crafts movement was the style that predominated the last decade of the nineteenth century. Major producers of textiles at this time were Morris and Co. (founded by William Morris) and Liberty and Co. Both companies drew heavily on floral motifs, especially Liberty, the majority of whose designs incorporated flowers, particularly poppies, anemonies, irises, tulips and lotus flowers, daffodils, lilies and wild roses. Petals and leaves merged together in lyrical swirls of repeated design, formalized pattern taking the place of cameo decorative motifs.

Floral decorative motifs were by no means limited to textile production. Arts and Crafts style extended to book covers, pottery, wallpaper and furniture. Art Nouveau, which was to take over in the early years of the twentieth century, retained the taste for flowers. Indeed, rambling roses, twisted ivy or nodding daffodil heads were to be found everywhere.

Colour was important to the Victorians. Pre-Raphaelite painting, whose heyday can be placed within the decade 1850-1860, replaced brown and earth colours with a brilliant, light intensified palette. Pictures of the rural idyll and classical romance were executed in the minutest detail and charged with emotion by vivid colouration.

In the home more brilliant colours were introduced with the advent of chemical or analine dyes. Purple, sage green, maroon, Prussian blue and mahogany took over where crimson had left off. Meanwhile, in the garden Jekyll was using white to punctuate great swathes of yellow, orange and red, mixing purple-blues with grey, pink and pale primrose.

Introduction

Derived from the French word *découper*, which means 'to cut out', découpage is the art of decorating with cut out shapes, patterns and pictures. The cut-outs are glued to a suitable surface and subsequently varnished many times. With careful work and a little patience the cuttings and surface unite to create a new and convincing object.

Be it homespun or exquisite, necessity or sheer indulgence, découpage is engaging, addictive even. Of necessity its practitioners become collectors and hoarders. One dare not throw anything away. A print which appears dull and uninteresting in isolation may be just what is needed to offset another which is lively and bold. The success of a project depends as much on how the images are combined and set out as it does on the dexterity of the cutting and quality of the finishing.

Découpage can be delicate and painstaking or it can be simple and direct. It might be just something to fill a wet afternoon or a grand statement of taste and style. Whatever form a project takes, your creation will be unique. Given the same source material no two people will produce the same object. Découpage recycles and reinvigorates mass-produced images to produce one-offs.

Like so much else, the roots of découpage are to be found in the East. Paper making originated in China 2,000 years ago and from that followed paper cutting. When the East India Company opened trade routes to the East, European eyes could scarcely believe the beauty of Oriental lacquerwork.

Demand for this wonderful coloured and highly finished furniture led artists and artisans all over Europe to experiment with their own styles and techniques throughout the nineteenth century.

There was money to be made. Not a trick was missed. So it was that in the hothouse workshops and arteliers of Venice, Paris and later London, that a new decorative art form was born.

Frustrated by the cost and time involved in working with paint and gold leaf, master painters engaged apprentices to colour, cut and manipulate their original engravings and etchings. Early in his career the Rococo artist François Boucher worked as an engraver for Watteau, who in turn had studied in Venice.

Gradually the new art slipped away from the masters. By the time of Louis XVI lesser artists such as Pillement had carved out a very successful niche. Chinoiserie was much in vogue with the ladies of the French court. Hour upon hour was spent perfecting scissor-work.

Throughout the eighteenth century découpage flourished all over Europe and all the while, as printed material became cheaper to produce more and more people were able to try their hand.

It is no surprise that the Victorians fell so much in love with this art. The Industrial Revolution forged a new world of mass-production. What the old masters had come to dismiss as arte povera (poor man's art) could now in a sense fulfil its destiny. Newspapers and magazines brought about an explosion of printed material. Images were more widely available than ever before.

Découpage was the perfect Victorian pastime. It brought together many character-istics of the age – the mania for collecting, a certain sense of thriftiness and an overarching sentimentality which saturated the public imagination.

Queen Victoria herself kept a scrapbook as did many millions of her subjects. All across the Empire, ladies eagerly gathered the popular images of the day – hearts and flowers, birds, angels, children and cats.

This book introduces the novice to the Victorian art of découpage. Each book in the Victorian Découpage series spotlights a subject that was particularly popular at the time. The projects are designed with the beginner in mind, with simple step-by-steps to help you learn the basic skills needed. Once you have had a go at a few basic projects and mastered the techniques you will be ready to progress to bigger things – stools, chairs, a table perhaps.

Découpage may sound daunting to the beginner. But with a little patience and care the plainest of objects can be transformed into something exciting and creative. This book will help you on your way. Read and enjoy!

Materials

DÉCOUPAGE MATERIALS

PAPER

Victorian scraps were tailormade for découpage. 'Scrap' was the name given to sheets of die-cut and embossed chromo-lithographs. These images were of an astonishingly high quality. The accuracy of the die-cutting was such that scissors were barely needed at all.

Albums pasted up with collections of scrap became known as 'scrapbooks'. Queen Victoria herself is known to have been a keen scrapbook keeper. Scraps were also used to adorn screens, or 'scrapscreens'. This art form was particularly popular in Germany, Britain and the United States – indeed, one of the most famous manufacturers of scraps, Raphael Tuck, was based in Germany and New York.

Another art form using scraps and pictures that was a particular favourite with the Victorians was decalcomania. This involved gluing scraps to the inside of clear glass vessels – typically vases – and then coating them with whitewash or enamel.

We have chosen images that are ideal for the projects and in-keeping with the Victorian era, but there are endless supplies of prints and images available to suit all tastes – see the section on Sources and Suppliers for some useful addresses.

Books are of course an excellent source of material. Second-hand books and magazines in particular can yield all manner of pictures suitable for découpage. Similarly, remaindered or bargain books are a good source. Try the 'natural science' and 'history' sections.

Giftwrap and wallpaper is good for découpage. Choose only high-quality, thicker papers. These papers have the advantage of using repeated images, which is a great help for some projects. (See the section on Suppliers in this book for some useful addresses.)

Postcards can be used, but because of their thickness, it is often necessary to split the card using a razor blade or thumbnail. Alternatively, use more coats of varnish.

Magazines are a useful source, but again avoid those produced with cheaper paper. Newsprint is often unsuitable because of the ink on the reverse. Poke around in junk shops for bygone periodicals.

Photocopies are a brilliant way to plunder all kinds of archive, but check that you are not breaking any copyright on the material you are using and keep within the guidelines of the law. A good machine with quality paper will give you a high-quality black and white image for a fraction of the price of a print. Colour photocopies used to be of poorer quality but have now become just as good as black and white. Once again, repeat images are not a problem and cutting error need not be disastrous.

BLANKS

Blanks are the bases from which many items are made. It is possible to find blanks in many guises including hatboxes, candlesticks, table mats, novelty boxes and letter racks. These can be purchased either direct from a craft retailer or via mail order. Alternatively you may track down new 'unfinished' blanks at your local DIY store.

PAINTS, VARNISHES, BRUSHES

Here it is best to visit a specialist shop, where the precise materials required should be in stock (see the section on Suppliers in this book for some useful addresses). Many of the paint colours we have used for these projects come from the Farrow and Ball specialist paint range. Suppliers to the National Trust, Farrow and Ball produce excellent quality paints, many of which are replica historic colours. A wide range of sample pots are available from the manufacturer, which are ideal for smaller-scale projects.

Paint is used to colour bases, tint scraps and touch in designs. You can also use it to enhance a decoration – try turning your hand to painting scrolls or ribbons. Household emulsion paint is as good as anything for painting blanks. It is a good idea to buy a small selection of primary colours and then mix them as required. For finer work you will need to use good quality artists' watercolour or coloured pencils. Inks may be used too, but be careful, ink is a concentrated pigment! For some finishes, you will need artists' oil paint.

In this book we've used crackle varnish. This two-part varnish compound is readily available from craft shops or by mail order.

It's easy to use and you will find it very effective in giving your object that mellowed, aged look. Look out for the Applicraft varnish, which is water-based and extremely easy to use.

We have also used scumble glaze medium. Again, this is available from good arts stockists or via mail order. Scumble medium mixes with paint and gives an opaque glaze to the surface of an object, which can be either smooth or distressed.

Other varnishes you will need to have to hand are acrylic water-based varnishes – we've used Craig and Rose – and a good quality oil-based varnish.

And last but not least, you will need a pot or two of gold and silver paste. We've used Rub and Buff wax paste, which gives excellent coverage and buffs to a deep shine. Again, you can buy these items from good quality craft shops or via mail order.

GLUE

The most commonly used glue in découpage is water-soluble PVA glue. This vinyl glue will stick paper, cardboard and fabric and can be diluted to any strength: a dilution of 1 part water to 5 parts glue makes for the most useful mixture. PVA glue is widely available.

SUNDRIES

While each project in this book lists the specific materials you'll need, there are a number of sundries that are common to all the découpage projects. You will need:

- Manicure scissors/découpage scissors. a craft knife or scalpel.
- Household scissors.
- Tweezers.
- A cutting mat and pasting board (a thick cardboard sheet works just as well).
- Repositioning adhesive such as Blu Tack.
- Disposable household cloth and natural sponge.
- HB pencil.
- Paper kitchen towels.
- White spirit for cleaning brushes with oil-based paint.
- Soap for cleaning glue brushes.
- Glass jars with screw tops – for storing varnish and glue mediums.

BRUSHES:

- Decorator's brushes – 1-inch and 2.5-inch – for painting on emulsion and applying glue.
- Varnishing brush – keep a dedicated varnishing brush set aside for varnishing.
- artists' brush – no. 4 – for those delicate touches.

SAFETY AND YOU

The following helpful hints should ensure trouble-free sessions at the découpage table:

•1• Make sure your working area is well-ventilated, dust free and uncluttered. Avoid using extension cables or anything that can be tripped over.

•2• Cover your work surface with newspaper when painting, gluing and varnishing.

•3• Always wear an apron. Never wear fibre-rich clothing such as wool – fibres soon find their way into paint and varnish.

•4• Wear thin, well-fitting rubber gloves when working with varnish. Wear gloves at all times if you have particularly sensitive skin.

•5• Keep all materials away from naked flame.

•6• If you are working on a number of projects, invest in a cheap paper dust mask. This will protect your lungs against dust and paint fumes.

Lady's Desk Set

Desk sets come in various versions – for this project we've selected a simple pencil holder and memo block, but you might also like to try working with a wooden pencil box or a writing folder. Other desk accessories that could be given a make-over of découpage include paper knives, magnifying glasses, letter holders, desk tidies and box or lever arch files.

This is an easy project that can be successfully adapted for children, especially those collectors who take a pride in their little 'bits and pieces'. As well as using the floral images, young children might have scraps of their own that they would like to use. See if they have some special pictures that they would like to use to decorate their very own desk tidy pot.

WHAT YOU NEED

- One blank pencil pot (or any suitable container)

- One blank MDF memo block holder

- Dark green emulsion paint

- Floral images

- PVA glue

- Water-based (acrylic) eggshell varnish

- Soft muslin cloth

- Gold wax

WHAT YOU DO

•1• Wipe over the surfaces of the pencil pot and memo block holder with a slightly damp cloth to remove any dust.

•2• Paint all the surfaces with two or three coats of dark green emulsion paint, allowing the paint to dry thoroughly after each coat.

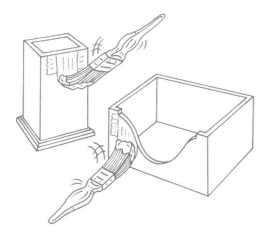

•3• Using a pair of sharp scissors, carefully cut out the floral images that you have selected, making sure none of the white background remains. You will probably need big, bold flowers for the pencil pot and smaller ones for the memo block holder.

•4• Position the flowers around the outside of the pencil pot and memo block holder to make sure fit and that the effect works well.

•5• Now place the scraps face down on a pasting board and coat with PVA/water-based acrylic glue.

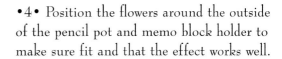

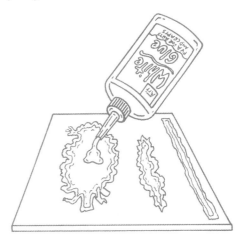

•6• Carefully firm down, making sure all the edges are stuck, then set aside to dry – this will take several hours.

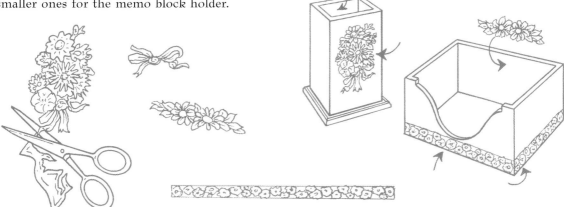

•7• Apply three or four coats of acrylic eggshell varnish to the entire surface area, allowing each coat to dry thoroughly before applying the next. Remember, the more coats of varnish that are applied, the longer the coats take to thoroughly dry.

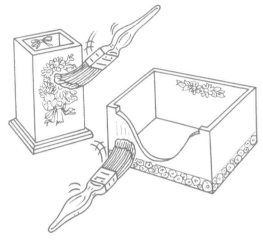

•8• Finally, using your finger apply a little gold wax to the top edges of the items. Remember, you will need to let the wax dry before you can use your items.

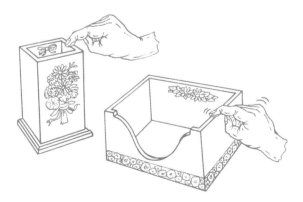

Hatbox

Hatboxes lend themselves to découpage as there are plenty of flat surfaces to cover. There is something rather exciting about a hatbox – you never quite know what will be inside. Use découpage to make your hatbox into a surprise – cover the inside surfaces with completely different scraps to those you've used on the outside and use a different, contrasting paint colour.

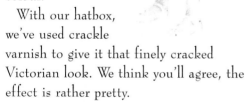

With our hatbox, we've used crackle varnish to give it that finely cracked Victorian look. We think you'll agree, the effect is rather pretty.

WHAT YOU NEED

- One blank cardboard hatbox

- Deep pink emulsion paint (for example Farrow & Ball Porphyry Pink)

- Cream emulsion paint

- A selection of floral images

- PVA glue

- Water-based (for example, acrylic) matt varnish

- Two-part crackle varnish (base coat and top coat)

- Artist's oil paint – raw umber

- Small piece of muslin cloth

- White spirit

- Oil-based matt varnish

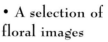

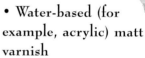

WHAT YOU DO

•1• Using a soft brush clean the surfaces of the hatbox to remove any dust.

•2• Paint the base of the box with a coat of deep pink emulsion paint and the lid with a coat of cream emulsion paint. Allow the paint to dry thoroughly and then repeat (you may need to leave overnight).

•3• Select the images you want to use, carefully cut them out and arrange them carefully until you are happy with the effect.

•4• Place the images on a pasting board and apply PVA glue to the backs, making sure not to over-glue. Stick the images onto the surfaces of the hatbox, making sure that all the edges are stuck down and that there are no air bubbles.

•5• Leave to dry (you may need to leave overnight).

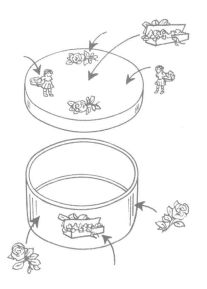

•6• Now apply three or four thin coats of water-based/acrylic matt varnish to the base of the hatbox. Make sure each coat is thoroughly dry before applying the next – a minimum of two hours between coats is probably all that is necessary, although you may find that the third and fourth coats take longer to dry than the previous coats.

•7• When varnishing make sure your working area is well ventilated and as dust free as possible. Keep a brush set aside especially for varnishing and look after it well – you don't want stray hairs in the varnish!

•8• Apply just one coat of water-based/acrylic matt varnish to the lid of the hatbox and leave until thoroughly dry.

•9• Next paint on two coats of the crackle varnish base coat, allowing the first coat to dry completely before applying the second.

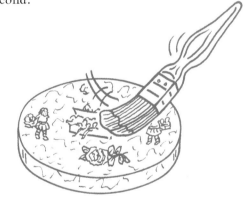

•10• When the second coat is dry, apply an even layer of crackle varnish top coat. You may find it necessary to warm the pot slightly by standing it in a shallow bowl of warm water, as this will make the varnish easier to spread.

•11• You now need to wait for the top coat to dry – this may take some time (anything from 6 to 24 hours), so be patient! As time goes on, a layer of fine cracks will appear on the surface.

•12• Dampen the muslin cloth with white spirit and squeeze out a pea-size amount of oil paint onto it. Rub the pigment over the crackle varnish and watch as the cracks are revealed. Make sure not to use too much paint.

•13• Set the lid aside for a further 72 hours until completely dry.

•14• Lastly, apply a thin coat of oil-based varnish over both the hatbox base and lid. This will protect the surface.

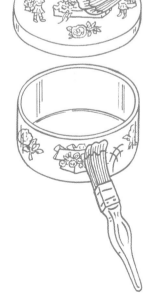

Picture Frame

Pretty as a picture, that's what a picture frame could be once you've given it a treatment of découpage. With your newly learnt skills, you could transform this simple object into something really special – a picture frame with real value added.

Picture frames are easy to get hold of. You can buy them from DIY stores, art and craft shops and gift shops. It's also worthwhile rummaging around your local bric-a-brac or antique shop, as they may have old frames for sale, often for not much money. Of course, if you buy an old frame, you will need to thoroughly clean it first – this may involve completely stripping it of any varnish or surface treatment.

24

WHAT YOU DO

•1• Remove the glass, backing and mount and clean the surface of the frame with a soft brush to remove any dust and dirt.

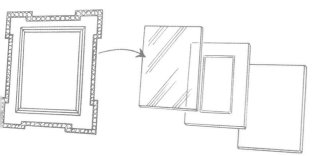

•2• Paint the entire surface with two or three coats of cream emulsion paint, allowing the paint to dry thoroughly after each coat.

•3• Using manicure scissors, carefully cut out the tulip images, making sure none of the white background remains.

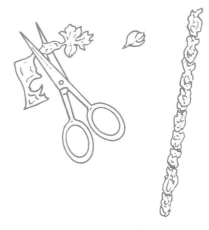

•4• Position the border and other images on the frame and adjust until you are happy with the effect.

•5• Now place the scraps face down on a pasting board and coat with PVA/water-based acrylic glue. Position them on the frame – you may find a pair of tweezers handy for those fine adjustments.

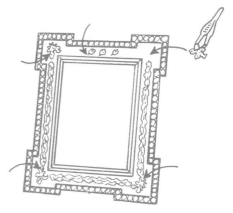

•6• Carefully firm down, making sure all the edges are stuck, then set aside to dry – this will take several hours.

•7• Apply three or four coats of acrylic matt varnish to the entire surface area, allowing each coat to dry thoroughly before applying the next. Remember, the more coats of varnish that are applied, the longer the coats take to thoroughly dry.

•9• Finally, using your finger apply gold wax to the inner edge of the frame.

•8• Once the final coat is dry, rub antique wax over the entire surface using a soft cloth. Buff to a soft sheen. You will find the wax gives the surface a subtle slightly aged look.

•10• Leave until completely dry, then reassemble the frame – don't forget to insert your favourite picture or photograph first!

Watering Can and Terracotta Pot

If you want to make an impression, try your hand at this more advanced project. Here we've transformed two everyday objects, a watering can and a flower pot, into an elegant complementary couple.

Your local garden centre or homecare store will provide the raw materials for this project – one plain galvanized watering can (any size will do), and one terracotta flower pot (again, of any size). Once you have primed the surface of the metal, you will find the working surface of the can no different to any other surface described in this book. You may find the terracotta rather more difficult to paint however, as the surface is highly porous, but with a little perseverance the paint will take.

WHAT YOU NEED

WATERING CAN

- One galvanized watering can

- Red oxide metal primer (available from your local DIY store)

- Dark green emulsion paint – darker colours are best for this project

- Floral images

- PVA glue

- Water-based (acrylic) eggshell varnish

- Oil-based eggshell varnish

- Antique wax – medium oak

- Gold wax paste

28

TERRACOTTA POT

- One terracotta pot

- Dark green emulsion paint

- Dark red emulsion paint

- Household wax candle

- Medium grade wire wool

- Muslin cloth

- Floral images (see back of book)

- PVA/water-based acrylic glue

- Water-based (acrylic) eggshell varnish

- Antique wax – medium oak

- Gold wax paste

WHAT YOU DO

WATERING CAN

•1• Wipe down the surface of the watering can to remove any dust and grease (you may need to use a little white spirit). Leave to dry.

•2 First apply a coat of red oxide metal primer to the outer surface of the watering can, making sure to follow the manufacturer's instructions. There is no need to prime or paint the inside of the watering can.

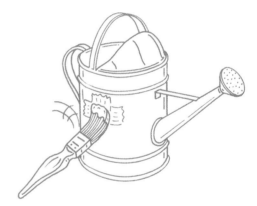

•3• When the surface is dry, paint with two coats of good quality dark green emulsion paint, making sure you have completely covered the oxide. Set aside to dry after each coat.

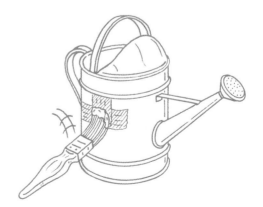

•4• Select your floral images and carefully cut them out. Position them on the surface of the watering can and adjust them until you are happy with the effect.

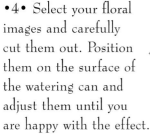

•5• Place your scraps face down on a pasting board and give them a generous coating of PVA adhesive glue. Carefully press them onto the surface of the watering can and firm them in place. You may need to snip the edges of some scraps to ease them flat on curved areas.

•6• Now apply three coats of acrylic eggshell varnish, allowing each coat to dry out thoroughly – you will find that the more coats you apply, the longer your object takes to dry out.

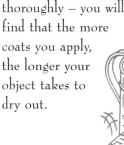

•7• Apply a final coat of oil-based eggshell varnish to help make the surface more water-resistant.

•8• Finally, a coat of antique wax adds a beautiful ageing sheen to the finished item.

TERRACOTTA POT

•9• Brush down the surface of the pot to remove any dust and grit.

•10• Apply two coats of dark red emulsion paint to the outside of the pot, allowing the first coat to dry out thoroughly before applying the second.

•11• When thoroughly dry, rub over the entire surface with the wax candle.

•12• Now paint the outer surface with two coats of dark green emulsion paint, completely covering the red paint and candle wax.

•13• Once the green paint is dry, rub the surface lightly with medium grade wire wool. By doing this you gradually expose the red paint underneath, giving the pot a distressed look.

•14• When you are happy with the effect, wipe the surface of the pot with a damp cloth to remove all dust.

•15• Now select and cut out your floral images. Position them around the pot, just under the rim.

•16• Place the scraps on a pasting board, apply PVA adhesive and carefully paste them in place. Gently firm them down, making sure to remove any air bubbles. Set aside and leave until completely dry.

•17• Apply three or four coats of water-based acrylic eggshell varnish, allowing each coat to thoroughly dry out each time (this will take between three and six hours minimum).

•18• Finally, apply a coat of antique wax to give your terracotta pot that elegantly aged look.

•19• Put your watering can and terracotta pot together, stand back, and admire your handiwork!

Floral Trough

A planter and a floral motif is an obvious combination, and one that can be particularly striking. By selecting flowers whose colours contrast with the background paint colour, a dramatic effect can be created. Once finished, you can fill the planter with matching flowering plants to further enhance the effect and heighten the drama!

This project uses a wooden planter for its base, and so you will need to keep the finished article for use inside the house. If you intend using it for small pot plants, you will need to make sure you protect the base of the planter so that it does not become damaged when watering. One way of doing this is to place the pot on a small dish (a jam jar lid will do nicely as well).

WHAT YOU NEED

- Blank wooden planter (search art and craft shops and mail order suppliers for a design you like)

- Pale green emulsion paint (see Farrow & Ball Cooking Apple Green)

- Pale yellow emulsion paint (Farrow & Ball Hound Lemon)

- Mid-tone yellow emulsion (Farrow & Ball Grevase Yellow)

- Natural sponge

- Acrylic scumble glaze (available from art shops and mail order suppliers)

- A selection of floral images

- PVA glue

- Water-based (for example, acrylic) matt varnish

WHAT YOU DO

•1• Thoroughly clean the surface of the planter inside and out to remove any dust.

•2• Paint the inside with two coats of pale green emulsion paint. Allow the paint to dry thoroughly between coats.

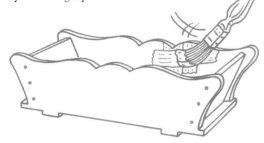

•3• When painting, work the paint in short cross-hatch strokes to ensure even coverage: do not be tempted to brush all one way. You will find it easier if you paint the sides of your vessel or container first, with your free hand holding down the base.

•4• Paint the outside of the planter with two coats of mid-tone yellow emulsion paint. Again, allow each coat to dry thoroughly.

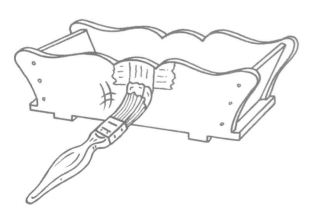

•5• On a plate mix a small amount of pale yellow emulsion paint with a small amount of scumble glaze and mix well. You are working to a ratio of 1 part paint to 1 part scumble – the consistency you require is rather like that of single cream.

•6• Dampen a small piece of natural sponge and dab it into the glaze, squeezing it gently against the sides of the plate until the sponge has an even coating of glaze. Use some kitchen paper to dab out any surplus glaze.

•7• Now using a gentle circular motion apply the glaze to the surface of the planter. It is a good idea to practise this application method first on a scrap of paper. The scumble glaze adds an aged patina to the surface of the object.

•8• Leave until completely dry – this can take several hours.

•9• Now take your floral images, place them on a cutting board and carefully cut them out using a sharp craft knife. You will need to take extra care around some of the details.

•10• Apply PVA glue to the backs of the images and position them around the planter. Firm them in place using a clean dry cloth, then set the planter aside until the glue is completely dry – this can take at least 12 hours.

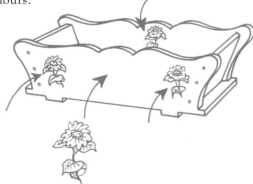

•11• Lastly, apply three or four coats of water-based/acrylic matt varnish to both the inside and the outside of the planter. You will need to allow each coat to dry thoroughly before applying the next – between three and six hours minimum.

•12• Once dry, your planter is ready to be filled with flowers and placed somewhere for everyone to see.

Candle Shade

A candle shade or lampshade is a particularly rewarding project. There is something quite magical about seeing your work of art illuminated with bright light, the découpage almost becomes alive!

Candle shades come in all sorts of shapes and sizes and are made of all sorts of materials, from cloth to metal. For this project we've chosen a pretty scallop-edged shade made of card, which is by far the easiest surface to work with, requiring minimal preparation. You should be able to track down a card shade in any quality high street DIY store or craft supplier.

We think you'll agree that flowers look splendid on this lamp shade. But they are by no means your only choice. For a child's room you might like to use teddy bears, cats or angels instead.

- **One blank cardboard candle shade**

- **A selection of floral images**

- **PVA glue**

- **Water-based (for example, acrylic) matt varnish**

- **Two-part crackle varnish (large cracks base coat and top coat)**

- **Artist's oil paint – lilac colour**

- **Small piece of muslin cloth**

- **White spirit**

- **Oil-based eggshell varnish**

WHAT YOU DO

•1• Using a soft brush clean the surfaces of the candle shade to remove any dust.

•2• Select the images you want to use, carefully cut them out and arrange them carefully until you are happy with the effect.

•3• Place the images on a pasting board and apply the backs with PVA glue, making sure not to over-glue. Stick the images onto the front of the candle shade, making sure that all the edges are stuck down and that there are no air bubbles.

•4• Leave to dry (you may need to leave overnight).

•5• Now apply one sealing coat of water-based/acrylic matt varnish to the front of the shade. Leave to dry – two hours should be long enough.

•6• When varnishing make sure your working area is well ventilated and as dust free as possible. Keep a brush set aside especially for varnishing and look after it well – you don't want stray hairs in the varnish!

•7• Next paint on two coats of the crackle varnish base coat, allowing the first coat to dry completely before applying the second.

•8• When the second coat is dry, apply an even layer of crackle varnish top coat. You may find it necessary to warm the pot slightly by standing it in a shallow bowl of warm water, as this will make the varnish easier to spread.

•9• You now need to wait for the top coat to dry – this may take some time (anything from 6 to 24 hours), so be patient! As time goes on, a layer of fine cracks will appear on the surface.

•10• Dampen the muslin cloth with white spirit and squeeze out a pea-size amount of oil paint onto it. Rub the pigment over the crackle varnish and watch as the cracks are revealed. Make sure not to use too much paint.

•11• Wipe away any excess paint, then set the shade aside for a further 72 hours until completely dry.

•12• Lastly, apply a thin coat of oil-based eggshell varnish over entire outer surface of the shade. This will protect the surface.

•13• Leave until completely dry, then assemble using a suitably complementary base. Splendid!

Keepsake Box

Découpage is all about transforming an object into something that is unique and special to you. Here's an object that you can not only recreate as a personal work of art, but can then use to store those things that are most precious to you – letters, postcards, photographs, mementos of a favourite holiday or special place, keepsakes given by someone you love.

For this project we are using a purpose-made keepsake box made from MDF, but you can also use various cast-off packaging such as shoe boxes and hat boxes – anything that is sturdy and has a fitted lid.

WHAT YOU NEED

- One blank MDF box with lid

- Fox-red emulsion paint

- A selection of floral images

- PVA glue

- Two-part crackle varnish (large cracks base coat and top coat)

- Oil-based matt varnish

- Artist's oil paint – gold

- Small piece of muslin cloth

- White spirit

WHAT YOU DO

•1• Using a soft brush clean the surfaces of the box and lid inside and out to remove any dust.

•2• Paint all the surfaces of the box and lid with a coat of fox-red emulsion paint using a small decorator's brush. Set aside to dry, then paint all the surfaces again.

•3• Select the images you want to use, carefully cut them out and arrange them around the sides of the box and on top of the lid until you are happy with the effects. You could also apply a motif to the inside of the lid, for a little extra surprise.

•4• Place the images on a pasting board and apply the backs with PVA glue, making sure not to over-glue. Position carefully and firm in place.

•5• Leave to dry (you may need to leave overnight).

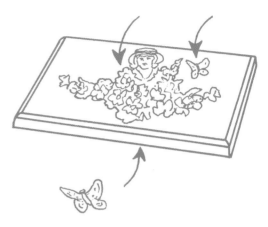

•6• Next paint on two coats of the crackle varnish base coat to all the surfaces, allowing the first coat to dry completely before applying the second. (See manufacturer's instructions for drying times.)

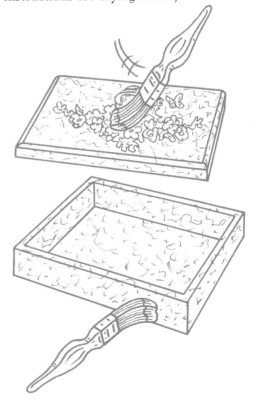

•7• When varnishing make sure your working area is well ventilated and as dust free as possible. Keep a brush set aside especially for varnishing and look after it well – you don't want stray hairs in the varnish!

•8• When the second coat is dry, apply an even, thin layer of crackle varnish top coat. You may find it necessary to warm the pot slightly by standing it in a shallow bowl of warm water, as this will make the varnish easier to spread.

•9• You now need to wait for the top coat to dry – this may take some time (anything from 6 to 24 hours), so be patient! As time goes on, a layer of fine cracks will appear on the surface.

•10• Now moisten a muslin cloth with white spirit, then squeeze out a pea-size amount of gold oil paint onto it. Rub the pigment over the crackle varnish and watch as the cracks are revealed. Make sure not to use too much paint.

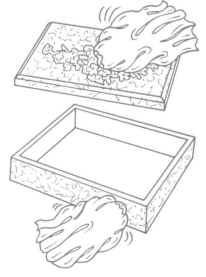

•11• Wipe away any excess paint with a dry cloth, then set the boxes aside for a further 72 hours until completely dry, making sure to leave them in a cool, well ventilated room.

•12• Lastly, apply a thin coat of oil-based matt varnish over all the surfaces. This will protect the boxes and make sure the crackle varnish is not damaged.

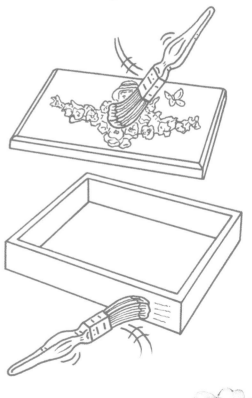

Key Cupboard

This project is good for the more advanced découpeur, who wishes to turn their hand to something a bit more challenging. Transforming plain and simple pieces of household furniture is very rewarding, as the Victorians found out. They lavished much time and energy on transforming sideboards, dressing tables, bedsteads and fire screens, and much of what they created still survives today. Perhaps your own work will also survive the test of time to be enjoyed by forthcoming generations!

Key cupboards such as the one we've used are fairly easy to find – try your local craft shop or DIY superstore. Mail order suppliers also stock them. As an alternative, you might be able to track down an old cupboard in a junk or antique shop – be sure to give it a thorough clean first, however, to remove all traces of paint, grease or dirt.

WHAT YOU NEED

- **One blank key cupboard (we've used a blank made of chipboard)**

- **Off-white/cream emulsion paint**

- **Floral images**

- **PVA glue**

- **Water-based (acrylic) matt varnish**

- **Gold wax paste**

WHAT YOU DO

•1• Make sure that the surfaces of the key cupboard are thoroughly clean before starting work. If there is any roughness, take some time to smooth it off using fine-grain sandpaper. Use a damp cloth to wipe over any prepared surfaces.

•2• Paint the entire cupboard with two or three coats of off-white emulsion paint. Allow each coat to dry thoroughly. It is a good idea to remove the hooks before doing this.

•3• Select the floral images that you wish to use and carefully cut them out. Position them on the door of the key cupboard until you are happy with the effect.

•4• Paste the scraps into position using PVA/water-based acrylic glue. Set aside to dry – this will take several hours.

•5• Now apply three or four coats of acrylic matt varnish to the entire surface of the cupboard, inside and out, allowing each coat to dry thoroughly – remember, the more coats of varnish that are applied, the longer the coats take to dry.

•6• Lastly, apply a small amount of gold wax paste to the knob and raised surfaces of the cupboard door for added emphasis. Set aside to dry – this takes around two hours – then buff to shine.

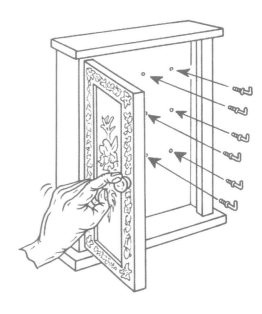

•7• Screw the hooks carefully back in place and your mini-masterpiece is now complete.

Tissue Box Cover

Tissue box covers are a popular choice with découpage beginners. Blank boxes are available from any good craft store or mail order catalogue. Their flat, simple surfaces make them easy to work with. With this project, nothing could possibly go wrong!

We've used flowers to decorate our tissue box cover, but it might also be fun to try out other themes as well, such as children's toys or angels – after all, you always need a tissue box in a nursery or children's play room.

- One blank square tissue box cover

- Bright-white/apple white emulsion paint

- Cooking-apple green emulsion paint

- Flower images

- PVA glue

- Acrylic scumble glaze medium (available from any good art or craft shop or mail order supplier)

- Masking tape

- Natural sponge

- Water-based (acrylic) matt varnish

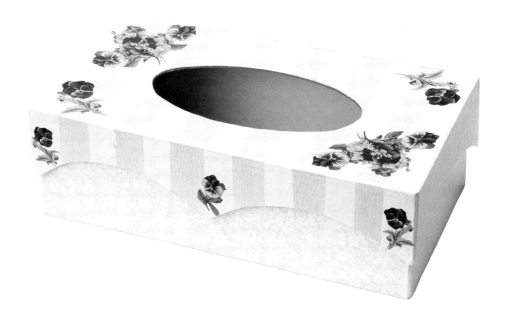

WHAT YOU DO

•1• Take a dry, clean brush and gently clean the surfaces of the box to remove any dust.

•2• Paint all the outer surfaces of the tissue box cover with two coats of new white emulsion paint. Allow each coat to dry out thoroughly.

•3• Paint all the inner surfaces with two coats of apple-green emulsion paint, allowing each coat to dry out thoroughly – this may take several hours.

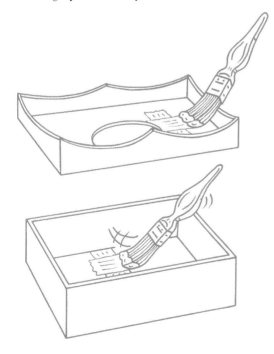

•4• Take an old clean plate and on it mix 1 tablespoon of green emulsion paint with 2 tablespoons of scumble glaze medium.

•5• Position strips of masking tape across the lid of the box, making sure they are evenly spaced. Using a one-inch decorator's brush, paint the exposed strips with the apple-green glaze mix, making sure your strokes are bold and consistent. This will create a dragged stripe effect.

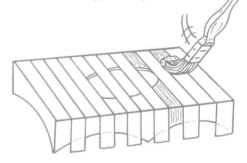

•6• When the glaze is completely dry, carefully remove the masking tape.

•7• Now take a slightly dampened natural sponge and dab it in the remaining scumble glaze mixture. Remove any excess paint from the sponge onto some kitchen paper.

•8• Apply glaze to the sides of the tissue box using a gentle dabbing motion to create a muted stippled effect. Make sure you don't use too much glaze, you are after a subtle broken effect, not a solid overall colour.

•9• Set the tissue box aside until it is thoroughly dry.

•10• Now you can select your images and carefully cut them out.

•11• Place the scraps on the top of the tissue box until you are happy with your arrangement.

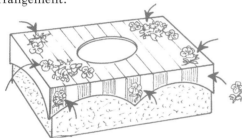

•12• Once the arrangement is right, apply PVA/water-based adhesive to the backs of the scraps and paste them into place. Set the box aside and leave it to dry – this will take several hours.

•13• Now apply three to four coats of acrylic matt varnish to the lid of the box, and one or two coats to the sides.

•14• Allow each coat of varnish to thoroughly dry before applying a further coat. (See manufacturer's instructions for recommended drying times.)

Glass Vase

Découpage glassware was extremely popular in the eighteenth and nineteenth centuries. Vases, in particular, were a great favourite, and were decorated with stunning results, artists often combining découpage with painting and gilding. Glass plates and bowls were also decorated in a similar way. Many of those that survive have now become collectors' items, achieving impressive prices in the salerooms.

You will need to remember one simple fact to successfully work with glass – this time you are working in reverse. Instead of sticking your images on top of an object, you are placing them glue-face up on the underside of the surface, then varnishing under instead of over them.

WHAT YOU NEED

- **One plain glass vase – wide-rimmed**

- **Floral images**

- **PVA glue**

- **Water-based (for example, acrylic) matt varnish**

- **Pale green emulsion paint**

WHAT YOU DO

•1• First select a suitable vase. You will need to find one that has a large enough neck for you to get your hand inside.

•2• Clean the vase in warm soapy water to remove any grease marks or stains. Allow to dry naturally.

•3• Carefully cut out the images you have selected and apply PVA adhesive to the front (printed) faces of them.

•4• Position each image on the inside of the vase so that the printed faces are clearly visible. You may find tweezers useful for those finer adjustments. It may also be necessary to clip some of the edges

to ease the image down flat on the curved surface – tiny snips should be all that is required.

•5• Press down the images using a dry muslin cloth and remove any air bubbles. Wipe off any excess glue with a damp cloth and then leave the vase to dry.

•6• Next paint over the entire inside surface with pale green emulsion paint, coating both the backs of the images and the remaining glass. Set aside to dry, then apply a second and third coat, allowing the paint to dry out thoroughly each time.

•7• Now apply two coats of acrylic matt varnish over the entire inside surface to seal the paint. You will need to allow the first coat to dry thoroughly before applying the second coat (around 6 hours).

•8• Your vase is now finished. A word of caution, however. Do not put water inside your découpaged vessel, as this will spoil the surface. If you want to use the vase to display cut flowers, you will need to stand a discrete plastic holder (a cut plastic bottle packed with florist's foam is ideal) in the bottom of the vase first, then arrange your flowers inside this.

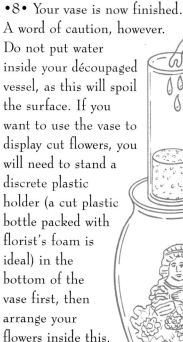

Sources and Suppliers

PAPER – UNITED KINGDOM

The suppliers listed below are useful sources for Victorian scraps, fine art giftwrap, fine art wallpaper, print-room borders and decoration and copyright-free designs.

Caspari Ltd
9 Shire Hill
Saffron Walden
Essex CB11 3AP
tel.: 01799 513010

The Dover Bookshop
18 Earlham Street
London WC2H 9LN
tel.: 0207 836 2111
Many of the images and scraps used in the projects in this book were reproduced by the kind permission of Dover publications.

Falkiner Fine Papers Ltd
76 Southampton Row
London WC1B 4AR
tel.: 0207 831 1151

Liberty and Co.
Regent Street
London WI
tel.: 0207 734 1234

Mamelok Press
Northern Way
Bury St Edmunds
Suffolk IP32 6NJ
tel.: 01284 762291

National Gallery Publications Ltd
5-9 Pall Mall East
London SW17 5BA
tel.: 0207 839 8544

National Trust Enterprises Ltd
36 Queen Anne's Gate
London SW1H 9AS
tel.: 0207 222 9251
(see also National Trust shops nationwide)

Paperchase Products Ltd
213 Tottenham Court Road
London W1P 9AF
tel.: 0207 323 3703

Past Times
Witney
Oxford OX8 6BH
tel.: 01993 770440
(see also Past Times shops nationwide)

A. J. Sanderson Ltd
52 Berners Street
London WI
tel.: 0207 584 3344

Scumble Goosie
Toadsmoor Road
Stroud
Gloucestershire GL5 2TB
tel.: 01453 731305

PAPER – UNITED STATES AND CANADA

Brandon Memorabilia
PO Box 20165
New York NY 10011
USA

Brunschwig & Fils
379 3rd Avenue
New York NY 10022
USA

Dover Publications
31 East 2nd Street
Mineola
NY 11501
USA
tel.: 001 516 294 7000

Flax Artists Materials
PO Box 7216
San Francisco
CA 94120-7216
USA
tel.: 001 415 468 7530

Laila's
1136 Lorimar Drive
Mississauga
Ontario L5S 1RY
Canada
tel.: 001 905 795 8955

Ornamenta
c/o C. Hyland
979 3rd Avenue
New York NY 10022
USA

A. J. Sanderson Ltd
979 3rd Avenue
New York NY10022
USA

PAINTS, FINISHES AND TOOLS – UNITED KINGDOM

The suppliers listed below are useful sources for
specialist fine art materials such as paint,
pigments, brushes, sealers, primers, glue, varnishes
and specialist sundries.

L. Cornelissen & Son Ltd
105 Great Russell Street
London WC1B 3LA
tel.: 0207 636 1045

Daler-Rowney Ltd
12 Percy Street
London W1A 2BP
tel.: 0207 636 8241

Farrow & Ball Ltd
Uddens Trading Estate
Wimborne
Dorset BH21 7NL
tel.: 01202 876 141

Foxwell and James
57 Farringdon Road
London EC1M 3JB
tel.: 0207 405 0152

J. H. Ratcliffe
135a Linaker Street
Southport PR8 DF
tel.: 01704 537999

Stuart R. Stevenson
68 Clerkenwell Road
London EC1M 5QA
tel.: 0207 253 1693

PAINTS, FINISHES AND TOOLS – UNITED STATES AND CANADA

Constantines
2050 East Chester Road
Bronx NY 10461
USA
tel.: 001 800 223 8087

Garrett Wade
161 Avenue of Americas
New York NY 10013
USA
tel.: 001 212 807 1155

Omer De Serres
334 Ste-Catherine East
Montreal
Quebec H2X IL7
Canada
tel.: 001 800 363 0318

Pearl Paint
308 Canal Street
New York NY 10013
USA
tel.: 001 800 221 6845

Sherwin Williams Canada, Inc.
170 Brunel Road
Mississanga
Ontario L4Z 1T5

Suppliers – Australia and New Zealand

Aidax Industries
64-68 Violet Street
Revesby
Sydney NSW 2212
Australia

Bristol Decorator Centre
76 Oatley Court
Belconnen ACT 2617
New Zealand

Golding Handcraft Centre
161 Cuba Street
PO Box 9022
Wellington
New Zealand

Oxford Art Supplies Pty Ltd
221-223 Oxford Street
Darlinhurst NSW 2010
Australia

Mail-order – United Kingdom

Mail-order companies are good sources of blanks, general craft sundries and fine art materials. Here are some useful addresses.

Fred Aldous
37 Lever Street
Manchester M60 1UX
tel.: 0161 236 2477
(arts and crafts)

The Box, Blank and Plaque Co.
D & S Crafts
Little Swineside
West Scafton
Leyburn
N. Yorks DL8 4RU
tel.: 01969 640617

Crafts and Collectables
1 Station Way
Cheam
Surrey SM3 8SD
tel.: 0208 288 0601
(arts and crafts)

Dainty Supplies Ltd
Unit 3
Phoenix Road
Crowther Ind. Est.
Washington
Tyne and Wear NE38 0AD
tel.: 0191 416 7886
(arts and crafts)

Janik Ltd
Brickfield Lane
Ruthin
North Wales LL15 2TN
tel.: 01824 702096
(arts and crafts)

MSA Crafts
Marvic House
Graingers Lane
Cradley Heath
West Midlands B64 6AD
tel.: 01384 568790
(arts and crafts)

Myriad Designs
PO Box 1
Prenton DO
Wirral L43 6XZ
tel.: 0151 652 5174
(blanks)

Smithcraft
Unit 1
Eastern Road
Aldershot
Hants GU12 4TE
tel.: 01252 342626
(arts and crafts)

USEFUL CONTACTS

Various craft organisations exist to help and support craftsmakers, both novices and the more experienced. Here are some useful addresses.

The Crafts Council
44a Pentonville Road
Islington
London N1 9BY
tel.: 0207 278 7700

(This nationwide organisation is a good place to start if you want to find out details of crafts societies and associations that exist locally. Alternatively, contact your Regional Arts Board, who hold databases of artists and associations and should be able to put you in touch with any local makers.)

Guild of British Découpeurs
18 Pembridge Close
Charlton Kings
Cheltenham GL5 6XY
tel.: 01242 235302

(Nationwide association which hosts regular meetings, workshops and exhibitions. Also produces bi-monthly magazine.)

National Guild of Découpeurs
5598 Forest View Drive
West Bend WI 53095
USA

(Worldwide organisation with chapters in Great Britain (listed above), South Africa, Australia, Canada and Japan.)

Index ❧══════════════════════════════════